Together or Apart?

Assessing siblings for permanent placement

Jenifer Lord and

Sarah Borthwick

BAAF
ADOPTION
& FOSTERING

Published by
British Association for Adoption & Fostering
(BAAF)
Saffron House
6–10 Kirby Street
London EC1N 8TS
www.baaf.org.uk

Registered charity 275689 (England and Wales)
and SCO39337 (Scotland)

© BAAF 2008
First published 2001
Second edition 2008

British Library Cataloguing in Publication Data
A catalogue record for this book is available from the
British Library

ISBN 978 1 905664 51 1

Designed by Andrew Haig & Associates
Typeset by Aldgate Press
Printed by Lavenham Press
Photographs on cover posed by models
from www.Istockphoto.com

BAAF is the leading UK-wide membership
organisation for all those concerned with adoption,
fostering and child care issues.

Contents

Acknowledgements

We would like to thank Adoption UK for putting us in touch with families who have adopted large sibling groups. We would also like to thank the families themselves for their very helpful comments and for their honest descriptions of what it's really like.

We are very grateful to the following people who made helpful comments and suggestions about the first edition: Sylvia Barker, Shelagh Beckett, Kate Cairns, Finola Culbert, Deborah Cullen, Cherilyn Dance, Marian Elgar, Bernadette Hermon, Mary Mather, Fran Moffat, Lexy Plumtree, Mo O'Reilly, Alan Rushton, Shaila Shah, Justin Simon, Gerrilyn Smith, Hannah Smith, Marcia Spencer and Teresa Stratford.

Notes about the authors

Jenifer Lord is a child placement consultant who has worked in BAAF's Southern region for many years. Before that she worked in a child care team and in an adoption and fostering team in two local authorities. She has written on a number of aspects of child placement. She has one brother.

Sarah Borthwick is an independent social work trainer and consultant. She formerly worked for BAAF as a trainer consultant and regional manager of the BAAF Southern region after which she was an adoption adviser to a local authority. She has three brothers and two sisters.

1 Introduction

Brothers and sisters who share a childhood and grow up together have potentially the longest lasting and one of the closest relationships of their lives with each other. The presumption should be that brothers and sisters will grow up together and every effort should be made to enable this to happen. Occasionally, for a variety of reasons, this is not possible or even desirable. However, the decision to separate brothers and sisters, or not to reunite or unite those who have become separated, should always be seen as one of crucial importance. It should be taken with great care and we hope that this guide will be helpful to those charged with this responsibility.

This guide focuses on the needs of brothers and sisters, individually and in groups, for whom a new permanent placement is the plan. It examines the legislative framework, research findings and practice experience in assessing and working with sibling groups. It highlights factors which affect decisions on whether brothers and sisters are placed together or separately and it considers when, how and by whom key decisions are made. Guidance is given about the assessment which is needed to aid planning and decision making.

The needs of new permanent families are considered and suggestions made about recruitment, preparation and support of families taking sibling groups. The actual process of placing brothers and sisters, including those who are to be separated and those who are to be united or re-united, is considered.

Finally, we discuss the issues around post-placement and post-adoption contact for siblings who are placed separately. Case studies are used to highlight practice dilemmas and good practice points.

Sibling is a convenient shorthand term and we have made use of it in the text. However, we are writing about brothers and sisters and we prefer this description. It is more powerful and means more to most people and we have used it as much as possible.

Nature and duration of sibling relationships

At least 80 per cent of the general population in the UK have one or more birth brother or sister. The relationship with these siblings starts from birth or early childhood and often endures into old age. It is usually a longer relationship than that with parents, children, or a partner. It is often intense and close in childhood. Siblings may then drift apart but often come together as adults and not infrequently, move to live together again in old age.

Brothers and sisters usually, but not always, share at least one birth parent and will also usually, but not always, have lived in the same family as children. However, they are often as different from each other in character and temperament as unrelated people.

Their experience of family life will have been different according to their position in the family, their gender, their ethnicity (if different from that of their siblings), their capabilities and their personality. They may have had quite different experiences from their siblings in the family and elsewhere and they may have perceived broadly similar experiences in a very different way. Their feelings for each other in childhood and over the years will probably have included a mixture of love, hate, jealousy, rivalry, like and dislike and there will almost certainly have been episodes of intense conflict as well as ones of joy, sharing and support. Many adults can remember occasions when they were deliberately unkind or even cruel to siblings as well as times when they felt closer to their brother or sister than to anyone else. If there are more than two siblings, there will probably have been shifting allegiances and groupings over the years. Siblings will probably have differing relationships with their parents and each child has almost certainly at some point felt that he or she was the least favoured one.

Siblings who are looked after

Children who are looked after are slightly more likely to have siblings than the general population. Estimates (summarised in Rushton *et al*, 2001) suggest that between 82 per cent and 87 per cent of looked after children have at least one brother or sister. However, virtually none of them are likely to be living with all their siblings. Some siblings may still be with family members or may be adult and living independently, but up to half of looked after children are placed separately from at least some of their siblings who are also looked after (Rushton *et al*, 2001). This is often because they have started being looked after at different times. It is quite often the case that one group of siblings is separated from another. It is estimated that at least half of all looked after children start being looked after with at least one sibling and the figure may be nearer 60 per cent of children under 11. Sibling groups currently represent over 50 per cent of referrals to BAAF's family finding services and just over 50 per cent of recent placements. Of all children adopted in England in 1998/9, 37 per cent were placed in sibling groups, 30 per cent in groups of two and 7 per cent in groups of three or more (Ivaldi, 2000). (Unfortunately, this is the latest available research which provides this detailed information.)

A definition of siblings

It is important to talk to children about who they consider their brothers and sisters to be. However, they may have siblings whom they are unaware of but who could become important for them. We suggest that a reasonable definition of siblings in childhood is as follows:

Children who share at least one birth parent

and/or

Children who live or have lived for a significant period with other children in a family group.

Many children live in complex family structures, with step-siblings and half-siblings living with them or elsewhere. However, looked after children often come from particularly fragmented and complex family networks. The following example is not untypical.

Case

Katie, aged nine, and her brother David, aged seven, have been in foster care together for five months, following several years of ultimately unsuccessful work with their parents and increasing concerns about their chronic neglect at home. Their infant brother, Andrew, who was born after they had left home, was removed at birth and has been in foster care for six weeks. He had to be placed separately as Katie and David's foster family was unable to accommodate a baby.

Katie and David's mother, Joanne, has a daughter, Michelle, who is now 17 and who has always lived with Joanne's mother. The grandmother also cares permanently for the disabled son of another of her daughters. Joanne also has a son, Jason, who is now 14 and who has lived since he was two with his paternal uncle and aunt. He is now on a Residence Order. Jason's uncle and aunt also have three birth children.

Joanne and her current partner Keith are the parents of Katie and Andrew. They also have two older children, Jamie aged 12 and Darren aged 11, who have been looked after for four years and who are currently in a permanent foster home. Their foster carers have two older birth children and have recently adopted a girl of five.

Joanne and Keith split up for a time, during which Keith had a daughter, now aged seven, who lives with her mother. He is also said to be the father of a two-year-old who has just been accommodated, although he denies he is the father.

During the separation, Joanne had a brief relationship and David was conceived. David's father, Robert, has daughters of 15 and 13 who live with their mother. He has also recently learned from an ex-girlfriend that he fathered a son, now 10, who was adopted as a baby. This child is believed to have joined a family who already had one adopted son. Robert is now in a stable partnership with Jackie. They have daughters of two and one and Jackie's daughter aged eight also lives with them. They have indicated that they would like to offer David a home, but not Katie or Andrew.

Kosonen (1999) describes "core" siblings as those with whom a child lives, and "kin" siblings as those living elsewhere with whom there is a more distant relationship. The reality, as illustrated in the above case, and as further described below, can be even more complex and it is important to explore this with each child.

David's closest sibling relationship is with Katie, with whom he has always lived. Katie has moderate learning difficulties and David is quite protective of her. However, he also feels close to his infant brother Andrew, whom he sees weekly and of whom he feels very proud. He is very aware of Jamie and Darren as his older brothers. His parents talked about them often although actual contact for David has not been frequent since his brothers were placed in foster care four years ago when he was three. He is quite wary of them and accepts that they seem

Family tree

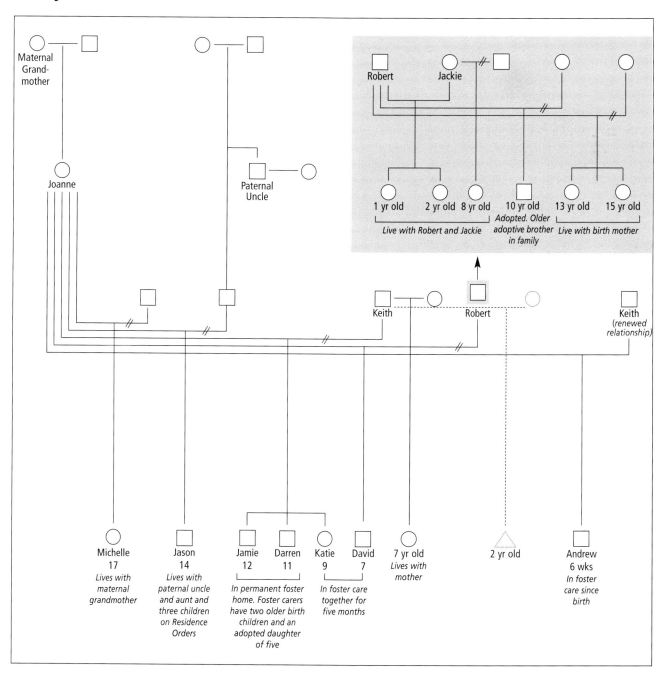

uninterested in him. David is, however, quite close to his oldest sister, Michelle, whom he sees on regular visits to his grandmother, with whom Michelle lives. David is only dimly aware of Jason and has never met him. He is completely unaware of his older siblings on his father's side – his two teenage sisters who live with their mother and his brother who was adopted as a baby. He has started having contact with his father since coming into care and he has just met his father's two young daughters and eight-year-old step-daughter and is quite interested in these newly acquired sisters. David, incidentally, has no "full" siblings. His parents, Joanne and Robert, had no other children together. All family members are white apart from Jason whose father is African-Caribbean.

This case illustrates some of the points which will be discussed later in more detail.

It is important to bear the following points in mind when planning placements for sibling groups.

- It is inevitable that many looked after children will grow up apart from at least some of their siblings, who are already settled in other families.

- It is important that as many siblings as possible are identified and that written information is gathered for children on their often complex family networks and scattered siblings.

- Extended family members should be considered first when looked after children need a new family and this should include non-related families parenting other siblings.

- If placement with adult family members will involve the separation of siblings currently living together, it should not be assumed that the link with the adult is more important than the link between the children.

- Separations of siblings purely because of a lack of immediate placement resources should not be allowed to become permanent.

- Arrangements for possible contact should be considered and discussed if children are unable to live with their siblings. These arrangements will need to be reviewed and revised over time.

- Agreements should be made with families, whether foster, adoptive or birth relatives, for them to be given updating information about siblings of the child whom they are parenting, and for them to give information on their child for the benefit of siblings.

- Agencies need clear policies and decision-making procedures in relation to siblings. Arrangements for post-placement and post-adoption contact and information-sharing are needed.

2 Law, policy and research

Law and policy

The law and guidance in the UK are clear that siblings should be placed together if possible and consistent with their welfare, and that contact between siblings should be considered should one or more of them be looked after and placed separately from others.

England and Wales

The main legal provision on the placement of siblings is contained in the Children Act 1989. This states that:

> where a local authority provide accommodation for a child whom they are looking after, they shall ... so far as is reasonably practicable and consistent with his welfare, secure that ... Where the authority are also providing accommodation for a sibling of his, they are accommodated together.
> (Section 23 (7) (b))

The Department of Health's guidance (DH, 1990) which accompanied the Act states that:

> Siblings should not be separated when in care or when being looked after under voluntary arrangements, unless this is part of a well thought out plan based on each child's needs. When large families require care away from home, every effort should be made to provide accommodation where they can remain together. However, a child's needs should not be sacrificed in order to meet those of a sibling.

Section 22(4) of the Children Act 1989 makes clear that:

> Before making any decision with respect to a child whom they are looking after, or proposing to look after, a local authority shall, so far as is reasonably practicable, ascertain the wishes and feelings of

> a) the child
> and
> 5) ... shall give due consideration –
> a) having regard to his age and understanding, to such wishes and feelings of the child as they have been able to ascertain.

Schedule 15 (1)c of the Children Act 1989 states that:

> Where a child is being looked after by a local authority, the authority shall, unless it is not reasonably practicable or consistent with his welfare, endeavour to promote contact between the child and ... c) any relative, friend or other person connected with him.

Schedule 7 to the Children Act 1989 prohibits the placement of more than three children with foster carers, unless a specific exemption is given. However, it allows this 'usual fostering limit' to be exceeded if the children are all members of the same sibling group.

The term "sibling" is not defined in the Children Act. It could include half-brothers and sisters, step-brothers and sisters or even unrelated children brought up as brothers and sisters.

Section 1 of the Adoption and Children Act 2002 requires the court and adoption agency, when coming to a decision relating to the adoption of a child, to have regard to 'the child's ascertainable wishes and feelings ...' (considered in the light of the child's age and understanding) and 'the relationship which the child has with relatives ... including ... the likelihood of any such relationship continuing and the value to the child of its doing so'.

The Adoption Agencies Regulations 2005 and Adoption Agencies (Wales) Regulations 2005 require a child's permanence report to be written when adoption is being considered as the plan. It must include information on the child's relationship with 'any brothers or sisters' he may have and 'the likelihood of any such relationship continuing and the value to the child of its doing so'.

The Adoption Support Services Regulations 2005 and the Adoption Support Services (Wales) Regulations 2005 allow financial support to be considered where it is desirable for the child to be placed with the same adoptive parent as his brother or sister, whether a full or a half sibling, or with a child with whom he has previously shared a home. (This includes single children joining siblings as well as siblings being placed as a group.)

LAC (98) 20, in Wales NAFWC 6/99, *Adoption – Achieving the Right Balance*, states that:

> *In the exceptional case where siblings cannot be placed together with the same family, it is important for agencies to ensure that contact arrangements with other siblings are given very careful attention and plans for maintaining contact are robust.*

In practice it will be hard to ensure that such plans are *legally* "robust". If the adopters of one child are or become averse to maintaining contact, it will be hard for any sibling to enforce contact by application to the court, even if this was thought to have been agreed. (See, for an example of an unsuccessful application for post adoption contact, *Re S [1998] 2 FLR 897*.) It is thus even more important to try and ensure that the adopters are genuinely committed to maintaining the sibling contact where this is considered desirable.

The Framework for the Assessment of Children in Need and their Families (DH, 2000) recognises that:

> *The quality of relationships between siblings may also be of major significance to a child's welfare.*

Article 8 of the Human Rights Act 1998 covers the right to respect for private and family life and prohibits interference with this. Family life in this context would certainly include siblings living together. Exceptions can be made to protect 'health and morals' and the 'rights and freedoms of others'. This clearly allows 'interference' in order to protect a child's right not to be subjected to harm by family members. Article 8 does reinforce the presumption that siblings living together should not be separated.

Scotland

Scots law is in the Children (Scotland) Act 1995 and the current supporting regulations, the Arrangements to Look After Children (Scotland) Regulations 1996. The 1995 Act does not specifically state that siblings must be placed together, but the 1996 Regulations say that local authorities must, so far as is consistent with their duties under s.17 of the 1995 Act and having ascertained the views of the children, place children in the same accommodation or 'as near together as is appropriate or practicable' (reg. 5(4)). In addition, Guidance from the Scottish Office in 1997 makes it clear that this should happen 'except where this would not be in one or more of the children's best interests' (*Scotland's Children* Vol 2, Chapter 1, para 19).

Section 17 of the 1995 Act says that the views of children and families must be considered so far as practicable, when any decision is being made about children who are or may be looked after.

For adoption placements, the 1997 Guidance (*Scotland's Children*, Vol 3, Chapter 1, para 12) says:

> *Wherever possible, therefore, except where it has been explicitly identified that siblings need to be placed separately due to coflicting individual needs, steps should be taken to secure an adoptive placement which can meet the needs of all the children in a family group together.*

In addition, reg. 3(2)(b) of the Adoption Allowances (Scotland) Regulations 1996 says that the possible placing together of siblings is one reason for considering an allowance. This is reinforced in the Guidance (*Scotland's Children*, Vol 3, Chapter 1, para 159). And the Adoption (Scotland) Act 1978 requires adoption agencies and courts to take account of the views of a child 'in reaching any decision relating to the adoption of a child' (s.6).

However, it should be noted that the Adoption and Children (Scotland) Act 2007 is expected to come into force in 2009, replacing the 1978 Act. The 1996 Regulations mentioned, including the ones for Looked After Children, and the 1997 Guidance will also be replaced with new provisions. The 2007 Act repeats the 1978 Act provisions about the views of children (s.14) and the new regulations and Guidance are expected to say much the same about the placing of siblings.

Northern Ireland

The relevant Northern Irish legislation is the Children (Northern Ireland) Order 1995. Article 27(8) states:

> Where a Trust provides accommodaton for a child whom they are looking after, they shall, so far as is reasonably practicable and consistent with his welfare, secure that –
> (a) the accommodation is near his home; and
> (b) where the authority is also providing accommodation for a sibling of his, they are accommodated together.

The DH circular dated May 1999, *Adoption – Achieving the Right Balance*, which gives guidance about permanency planning for children, states:

> In the exceptional case where siblings cannot be placed together within the same family it is important for agencies to ensure that contact arrangements with other siblings are given very careful attention and plans for maintaining contact are robust.

Research

Given that almost 90 per cent of looked after children are estimated to have siblings and that between half and two-thirds of children start being looked after with at least one sibling, it is surprising that issues in sibling placements have received relatively little research attention. One reason may be the complexity of defining and quantifying just who a child's siblings are, as described in the previous chapter. A BAAF study (Ivaldi, 2000) found that 37 per cent of all children adopted in England during 1998/9 were placed as part of a sibling group: 30 per cent in groups of two and 7 per cent in groups of three or more. Around 25 per cent of adoptive families had sibling groups placed with them. However, it is also estimated (see Rushton *et al*, 2001) that up to a half of looked after children have siblings not in the care system and up to two-thirds have at least some siblings placed separately from them in the care system, often children who have started being looked after at a different time. Children are often placed with some of their siblings

but have others, both in and out of the care system, from whom they are separated (see case example, Pg. 2).

Placement outcomes

Although there have been few studies whose main focus has been sibling placements, several wider studies have included comments on outcomes according to whether children are placed with siblings or not.

Rushton *et al* (2001) comment that:

> The majority of these studies have reported that sibling placements have tended towards better outcomes, either in being less likely to disrupt or in showing higher levels of new parent satisfaction or lower levels of child problems … . However, the findings are often complex and show both advantages and problems.

Hegar's international overview (2005) also reached the tentative conclusion that:

> Joint sibling placements are as stable, or more stable, than placements of single children or separated siblings, and several studies suggest that children do as well or better when placed with their brothers and sisters.

Wedge and Mantle (1991) found that the older siblings in a group placed together had a lower disruption rate than singly placed children of that age, while younger siblings had a higher disruption rate than singly placed children of their age. This suggests that a sibling group placement may sometimes "protect" an older child but may also put a younger sibling's placement slightly more at risk. They concluded that although many sibling placements are positive, they can carry additional risk and stress for carers.

Rushton *et al* (1989) found that boys placed with siblings 'made better progress than those placed alone, but the latter differed in having higher initial problem levels'.

Quinton *et al* (1998) found that outcomes were poorer for singly placed children and that this was particularly true when the child's siblings remained in the birth home and the placed child had experienced rejection by birth parents. Children scapegoated at home by parents but now placed with siblings did as well as their siblings.

Quinton et al also found there were poorer outcomes for singly placed children when they joined an established family. Difficulties between the placed children and the family's birth children were relatively frequent. This study confirmed the findings of others (Parker, 1966; Wedge and Mantle, 1991) that where the placed child was older or close in age to the youngest child, placements were more prone to poorer outcomes. However, in Quinton et al's study, sibling relationship difficulties occurred with wider age gaps too. They found that significant problems also arose when the birth sibling was an adolescent.

However, Beckett et al (1999), in their study of children adopted from Romania, found that the problems reported by adopters between children close in age appeared to reduce over the years.

Rushton et al (2001) indicate that being parented by an older sibling can be a protective factor for younger children. There is no comprehensive research finding on the effect this may have on the parenting child.

Farmer and Pollock (1998) focused on substitute care for sexually abused or abusing children. They found that siblings who were sexually abused were slightly more often separated from their brothers and sisters. They noted that often high levels of supervision were needed when siblings were placed together as there was a very real risk of sexual activity between the siblings (see also Elgar and Head, 1997; Macaskill, 1991). Farmer and Pollock (1998) further commented that 40 per cent of children who displayed abusive behaviour never saw their brothers and sisters. A number of children went on to sexually abuse "foster siblings" in placement. Often carers were unaware of the history of abusive behaviour.

In a study of contact in the adoption of younger children, Neil (1999) found that, even though many children were separated from siblings for a variety of reasons, there were often no arrangements made for contact between them after adoption. This was particularly the case for paternal siblings. It was less likely for there to be contact arrangements with siblings who remained within the birth family. There is further discussion of research findings in relation to contact in Chapter 8.

There is no research that we know of which looks at sibling groups who are separated after permanent placement because of the disruption of the placement of one of them. It would be helpful to know how often this happens, in what sort of situations, and what the effects are on children who leave and children who remain.

3 Factors which affect decisions about whether siblings should be placed together or separately

Introduction

Clearly each child's own wishes and feelings, the assessed quality of attachment between siblings, and each child's assessed needs are the most important factors which should inform decisions about whether siblings are placed in a permanent new family together or separately. Chapter 5 is devoted to a discussion of these factors.

However, there are also organisational, practical and financial issues which impact on decisions and these are outlined in this chapter.

Factors relating to individual children, such as their age, their ethnicity, their disability, their contact needs and the plan for them, can also affect whether they are placed on their own or with siblings and these are also discussed in this chapter.

Organisational issues

Policies and procedures

Clear, written policies and procedures can be helpful in ensuring some consistency in decision making. They can also facilitate speedy decision making. Delay can often occur when workers are unsure what to do next and have no clear guidelines on how to proceed and what policies and principles of good practice to take into account. We recommend that there should be specific written policies and procedures in relation to working with and planning for sibling groups. There should be a clear statement that consideration will always be given first to placing children with their siblings, if necessary by re-uniting or uniting them. There should be written procedures covering the factors to be taken into account when assessing siblings, the role of different decision-making forums, and the timescales for reaching decisions. It could, for example, be helpful to have a policy and procedure in relation to moving children as soon as a suitable vacancy occurs so that

siblings who have had to be placed separately on entry to care can be re-united. This may be a move which it is right to make and children, birth parents, foster carers, and social work managers need to be clear that this is a child-centred agency policy and is likely to happen.

Staffing issues

When siblings are in separate foster placements or some are still at home, there is a danger that there is inadequate consideration of them as a sibling group unless there is someone with an overview. It is important that consideration is given to one social worker having all the siblings on a caseload or, more practically, two (or more) social workers having responsibility for different members of the sibling group but working as a team, ideally with one overall team manager. One reviewing officer for all the members of a sibling group can be very helpful. There will also need to be close liaison if another worker, or even another team or local authority, has prime responsibility for working with other siblings who may still be at home or elsewhere in the extended family or the care system.

Personal beliefs of social workers, foster carers, panel members and other professionals

There needs to be an acknowledgement that many workers and others have strong views, often based on their own personal experience, about whether siblings should be kept together at all costs or should ever be separated. Some may find it impossible ever to contemplate siblings needing to be placed separately, while others may find it impossible to believe that any new family could parent a group of four or five siblings, all of whom are needy in their own right. This can be the case for those who have worked with or, indeed, been part of a large, chaotic, dysfunctional birth family and who have found the experience overwhelming. 'I can't imagine how anyone could possibly do it', was a comment made at the recruitment and preparation stage to a number of the subsequently successful adopters of large sibling groups to whom we spoke. Some people also differentiate quite markedly between "full" siblings and "half" siblings, even when such distinctions seem, or indeed are, unimportant to the children involved. Training and supervision are both important in enabling people to air and discuss their views and to consider possible alternatives. Clear policies and procedures and group working and decision-making are important checks and balances on personal beliefs.

Placement resources

Unfortunately, it is quite often the case that siblings are split on entry to care because there are no foster carers available to take the whole group. Children are then in danger of growing apart from each other. They may form strong attachments with their carers and it may then prove difficult or impossible to re-unite them with their siblings. It is essential that frequent contact is arranged for siblings split between different foster carers and that an assessment of the whole group takes place as soon as possible. Consideration should also be given to moving the children to a joint foster placement to facilitate this assessment, provided that this can be done quickly.

Sibling groups may also need to be split because of a lack of permanent new families able to take the group. Issues around the recruitment, assessment, preparation and support of foster and adoptive families are discussed in Chapter 6.

It is very important that local authorities monitor the sibling groups whom they look after and the resources available for them. They should also monitor carefully the use of both foster carers and adopters, some of whom may have single children placed with them when they could take sibling groups. Local authorities can then be clear about how often sibling groups have to be split because of a lack of appropriate families and can try and address some of the issues raised in Chapter 6.

Financial resources

There is discussion in Chapter 6 of the almost certain need for considerable practical and financial help if new families are to be asked to parent sibling groups. It is important, too, to budget for inter-agency fees and advertising costs, which may well be necessary. There will also be a need to invest in staff time, transport and other expenses involved in facilitating contact between siblings who are separated in temporary foster care.

If there are insufficient local task-centred foster family resources, agreement may need to be given, in the short term, to looking elsewhere, e.g. to voluntary organisations or independent fostering agencies, which may have families able to accommodate sibling groups.

Factors relating to individual children

Age

There can be a considerable age gap between siblings. Sometimes one of the children, often an older sister, has taken prime responsibility for "parenting" younger brothers and sisters. It can be particularly hard for the older child when this level of "parenting" is no longer needed and when younger siblings turn instead to their foster carers or adoptive parents. Careful work is needed with the "parenting" children to validate and praise the role they played when it was needed but to help them understand and accept that it is no longer needed in the same way and that they, too, have a right to be cared for. They may still have a valuable role as a "consultant" to the new parents, particularly in the early stages of a placement.

Clearly it would often be quicker to place younger children for adoption without their older siblings. However, the advantage of an earlier placement for them has to be carefully balanced against the life-time loss of the experience of growing up with their older sibling. Sometimes, depending partly on the degree and quality of attachment between the children, it may prove necessary to place younger children on their own if efforts to find a family for all the children have failed within set timescales. If this is the case, it is essential that clear arrangements for ongoing and meaningful contact are agreed.

There is some limited evidence from research (Wedge and Mantle, 1991) that being placed with younger siblings can be a protective factor for an older child, i.e. their placement is slightly more likely to be successful than for children of their age placed on their own. However, the same research shows that the obverse is true too, and that younger siblings are slightly less likely to have a successful placement when placed with older siblings.

Starting to be looked after at different times

Kosonen (1996) found that the most frequent reason for the separation of siblings was that they had started to be looked after at different times.

Sometimes this is inevitable; younger siblings may not even be born when older ones start being looked after. However, sometimes a decision is made to remove some children, often older ones, and to leave other children at home with parents. The possible long-term implications of this need to be very carefully considered. The separation of siblings who live together should be viewed as a decision which is at least as serious as the decision to separate children from their parents.

It is important to look on foster or adoptive families who are already parenting a sibling as "extended family" of a child now needing to be looked after, and to consider carefully whether the children could be re-united or united. They may never have lived together but a placement together would enable them to grow up as siblings and could be seen as an important investment for the future.

The preparation of all new permanent families should include some discussion of the possibility of a child placed with them subsequently having a sibling who needs placement. At the very least there should be an agreement that they would be told of this. The possibility of some contact, or even of a joint placement, could then be discussed. (See further discussion in Chapter 6.)

Legal status and plan

Particularly when there is quite an age difference between children, the plan may be different. Older children may be quite clear that they do not want to commit themselves to adoption while for younger children it is clear that a childhood in local authority care is not right and that adoption should be the plan. This difference in plan and in proposed legal status in the new family should not necessarily be a reason for placing siblings separately.

Direct work with children is essential, including involving them in the planning process and explaining the implications of each different legal status. Children can be helped to make sense of this. In fact, many families include both birth and adopted children. There may also be stepchildren and quite a number also include foster children.

An older sibling who has opted for fostering rather than adoption may eventually agree to either adoption, special guardianship or a residence order, particularly if he or she understands that they do not have to stop contact with their birth family and do not have to change their surname. It is important that there is discussion with families taking a sibling group, some of whom will be fostered and some adopted, about the possibility of older children eventually wanting adoption too. The financial implications of this need to be thought about and the family given some indication of what adoption allowances and other financial help might be available.

Contact needs

Children of different ages, with different plans, may also have different contact needs. There is a full discussion of issues arising from this in Chapter 8. Each individual child's contact needs must be assessed and it may well be that the plan is for siblings placed together to have different forms or amounts of contact. For instance, an older child may want and need more contact with a birth relative than their younger sibling. Children may also have different relatives, e.g. father and paternal relatives, who want to see one child but not another. This can work in new families, who may well have birth children or other unrelated adopted, fostered or stepchildren too. However, it places enormous demands on new families and practical, including financial, help as well as social work support may well be necessary. It may also be that older children have to agree some compromise in relation to contact with their birth relatives if this is necessary to ensure the safety and need for confidentiality of the younger siblings with whom they want to be placed. This may be accepted at the time but become a source of resentment later on. It is important that arrangements are reviewed and revised as the years go by.

Views and wishes of birth relatives

As discussed above, birth relatives may only want contact with "their" child in a sibling group or may want more contact with one child than another. While this may be able to be accommodated, work needs to be done with birth relatives to help them to understand and to accept as far as possible that their child is part of a sibling group and that it may not be helpful to any of the children to try and maintain a link with one child and to ignore the others.

Sometimes birth relatives wish to offer a home to one child but not to the others. The case described on Page 2 illustrates this.

> *David's father wants to parent David but feels unable to take on Katie and Andrew. A careful assessment will be needed and an acknowledgement made that David will experience a loss, whatever is decided. If he moves to live with his father, he will gain two younger half-sisters and an older step-sister but will lose the experience of being brought up with Katie, with whom he has always lived, and also the possibility of living with his brother Andrew. If he remains with Katie, he will lose the opportunity to be brought up by his father and with his younger sisters. Ongoing contact is likely to be essential whatever is decided and it might be possible, for instance, to include Katie as well as David, in contact with David's father's family, should a decision be made to keep David and Katie together.*

In other situations, birth parents often want a sibling group to be placed together in a permanent new family if they have to be placed at all. They may find it easier to accept the plan if they are reassured that the children are to be kept together.

Ethnicity

It is increasingly common for there to be sibling groups which include children of different ethnicities. For example, two children may have the same white English mother but one may have a white Irish father and one an African-Caribbean father. As with all siblings, the presumption should be that the children will stay together unless there is a good reason to separate them. As with all children, the most appropriate permanent new family is likely to be one which reflects the children's ethnicity as closely as possible.

For the children described above, this would be a family incorporating parents with white English and Irish and African-Caribbean heritage. However, if this specific link is not possible to achieve, it is particularly important to ensure that each child still has the opportunity 'to positively develop those

heritages that are most minimised or devalued in wider society.'* In our example above, the black child of mixed parentage in the group belongs to a minority ethnic group and will experience racism at some time in his or her life. It is particularly important, therefore, that a new family should include at least one black parent. Other black families of a different ethnicity may also be considered, provided they are assessed as able to meet the needs of the black child. Any family will also have to make efforts to ensure that the white child's Irish heritage is valued and actively promoted.

When assessing the holistic needs of each child, it will be important to explore how each one perceives his/her own ethnic identity and that of their sibling. In our example, has either child internalised a view from outside or from within their family about the value of an English, Irish or African-Caribbean heritage? Work with the children separately and together on these issues will be necessary before they can be placed in a permanent new family.

It is important to remember that a white child or a black child of mixed parentage is likely to retain access to dominant white role models and to their white heritage even if placed with a black family in the UK.

White parents are likely to find it significantly harder to meet the needs of a black child, including a black child of mixed parentage; such placements should remain exceptional. If they do occur, considerable efforts will need to be made by the agency and by the parents to ensure that, as far as possible, the parents and their wider family are able to value and actively promote the black child's racial, cultural and identity needs as well as meeting the needs of the child's white sibling.

Disability

It is as important, as with any other sibling group, to assess relationships between children and the functioning of the group as a whole as well as each child's individual needs when one child is disabled. Efforts should be made to ascertain the wishes, feelings and views of each child in the group. There should not be a pre-conceived view taken that a

---

* There is fuller discussion of these issues in *Race and Ethnicity* (Prevatt-Goldstein and Spencer, 2000) and in Prevatt-Goldstein's chapter in *We Are Family* (Mullender (ed) 1999).

disabled child needs a separate placement from siblings or, if siblings are to be split, that he or she should be the one to be placed on their own.

Sometimes there are groups of two or even more brothers and sisters, all of whom are disabled. There can be an assumption that a placement together would be neither feasible nor appropriate. Social workers need to be aware that their personal prejudices could be getting in the way of an objective assessment of the children's needs. There certainly are parents, sometimes single parents, who are successfully parenting several disabled children, albeit often children who have been placed individually.

Emotional and behavioural difficulties

A very common reason for placing siblings separately is when one is seen as having special needs in terms of their behaviour, their need for individual attention, and the demands which they are likely to make on new carers. An assessment may indicate that a particular child has such great needs that he or she should be placed on their own. There is often the fear that this child may jeopardise the permanent placement for the other children. It can be right to place a member of a sibling group separately, and this is discussed in more detail in Chapter 5. However, an assessment may indicate that a child currently displaying particularly difficult behaviour could be helped with some focused direct work or brief therapy while in their temporary foster home.

Kyle, aged five, is the eldest of four siblings. He and two of his siblings are of white English and white/African-Caribbean parentage. The youngest child is of white English and Scottish parentage. Kyle had spent longest at home and was displaying much more challenging behaviour than his younger siblings. Consideration was given to placing him on his own. However, he was offered some therapy sessions and was enabled to moderate his behaviour and to become more settled and less confused. He was placed for adoption with his siblings with a white and African-Caribbean family and, while he has proved more demanding to parent than they have, his adoptive mother now comments, 'I couldn't imagine the children without Kyle. It would have been tragic if he'd been separated from them.'

Experience of abuse

Experience of abuse should not be a reason for placing siblings separately before a thorough assessment has taken place. However, each child's safety and ability to recover from abuse, if still locked into an abusive pattern of behaviour with a sibling, needs to be carefully assessed, and may result in a decision to place siblings separately. This is discussed in more detail in Chapter 5. It also needs to be recognised that a child may take their "role" and their pattern of behaviour into a new family even if they have been separated from a sibling. Children displaying abusive behaviour can pose a risk to other children in placement and careful consideration needs to be given to placing some children in a family in which there are other children.

4 Planning for children in sibling groups:
When, how and by whom are decisions made?

Introduction

The decision as to whether or not to separate a sibling group on a permanent basis is a crucially important one. It will have lifelong implications for the children and should, in our view, be seen as having equal importance with the decision to separate children and parents. Decisions on whether or not to re-unite siblings who are already separated or to unite siblings who have never lived together, are equally crucial.

It is essential that:

- there is a clear and transparent process for arriving at the decision; and

- it is made following a group discussion to which everyone involved, including, of course, the children concerned, has had an opportunity to contribute in some way.

There may be discussions in various forums and these are detailed below. However, we recommend that the conclusions of these discussions should be taken to a review meeting, which may need to be specially convened, and that this is where a final decision of such importance should be made.

Written policies and procedures will be important in clarifying the factors to be taken into account, the role of different forums and the timescales for reaching decisions. Decisions should be informed by a critical assessment of established and any new research evidence. There is fuller discussion of this in Chapter 3.

Children in need assessment

A child's relationship with siblings, both those he or she is currently living with and those who may be elsewhere, should be a dimension of the work with the child from the time that the family first comes to the attention of social workers. The *Framework for the Assessment of Children in Need and Their Families* (DH, 2000) is clear that 'good relationships with siblings' is a factor to be taken into account in

assessing the child's developmental needs. In assessing family and environmental factors, another of the assessment dimensions, the history of the child's family, is seen as significant. This is seen to include absent wider family and could well include other children removed or separated from the family in the past. Who do the child and parents consider to be members of the wider family and what is their role and importance to the child and parents? It is noted that 'the quality of relationships between siblings may also be of major significance to a child's welfare' (DH, 2000).

It is important that an assessment of sibling relationships, as well as parent–child relationships, starts at this point, with analysis of how the group functions as a whole as well as the relationship of each individual child with the others and with parents. Is there a favoured child (or children)? Is there a scapegoated child? Is there a parenting child who takes responsibility for the younger ones? This will often, but not always, be the oldest child. Are boys and girls perceived differently in the family? How much are children modelling their behaviour on their parents or on older siblings? How much warmth and caring is there between siblings and how much conflict? Are siblings abusing each other, emotionally, physically or sexually?

The Assessment Framework (DH, 2000) states that:

> the child's responses and interactions in different situations should be carefully observed wherever possible, alone, with siblings, with parents and/or caregivers...

Clearly children's relationships with each other within a possibly very dysfunctional family will be distorted to some extent. However, it is vital to gather information on what is happening and to work, if necessary, as part of a family support package, on relationships between siblings as well as between parents and children. This will inform future work with children should they need to be looked after and will also inform crucial decisions about whether to remove all or only some of the children at one time.

Case

(See Pg. 2, where the case is first described.)

Jamie and Darren were removed from home when they were eight and seven, following several years of inadequate parenting and increasing concerns that the boys were alternating between running wild and then being severely punished by their father. When Jamie and Darren were removed, their younger siblings Katie, then aged five, and David, aged three, were left at home. They were seen as presenting fewer problems and seemed more compliant, placid children who were easier to parent. There was no real assessment of how the four children related to each other and of how each of them perceived the separation.

When Katie and David were removed four years later, the two older boys were settled on a permanent basis in what had been their short-term foster family and there was almost no contact with the younger children. David had almost no memory of Jamie and Darren but it emerged that Katie had missed them terribly and would have liked to have left home with them. Jamie had never had much time for his younger siblings and had modelled himself on his powerful, often violent father. Darren would seem, in retrospect, to have been quite close to Katie and sad that he no longer saw her. It now seems possible that this is one reason why he particularly resents the young girl whom his foster carers have adopted.

Care plan

It is essential that the care plan is clear about why some children are being looked after and others left at home, if this is the plan, and also about whether a joint permanent placement for the looked after children is the plan or not. If siblings have been separated, the plan should include detailed information on how contact between them is to be maintained.

Role of time-limited foster carers

Looked after siblings are quite often placed in separate foster families, either because they have started being looked after at different times, or because it has been decided that they would do best in separate families or, sadly but quite commonly, because of a lack of families available to take all the children.

Foster carers have a vital role, in these situations, in promoting and facilitating contact between the children, if this is the plan, and in participating in any assessment of whether siblings should be separated in a permanent placement or should be re-united or united with siblings for a permanent placement. Carers need training, help and support in doing this.

Practical support issues for families taking large sibling groups on either a time-limited or a permanent basis are discussed in Chapter 6. However, all families may be involved at some point in hosting or being involved in meetings between siblings, which may require additional practical support.

Foster carers need to be able to work as part of a team with other foster carers and social workers. It can be helpful if relationships have already been built up through a local foster carer group or perhaps between small local clusters of foster families getting to know each other so that they could, if necessary, offer a service to a number of siblings between them.

Foster carers have a very important role in the assessment of whether siblings in their care should remain together in a permanent placement or be split. However, this should be part of a well thought-out assessment plan. It should be made clear to foster carers that, until a definite decision based on a thorough assessment has been made to split siblings, they remain together. Siblings should not be split simply because an individual foster family cannot manage the care of one of them or wants to permanently keep one or more but not all of the children. This will be important information for the assessment, and assessments should be done as quickly as possible, but it should be agreed with carers that decisions about splits cannot happen otherwise, other than in exceptional circumstances. It may well be necessary to remove all the siblings, rather than allow them to be split in this situation, even if this means going outside the local authority's own resources to find a foster family or even a small residential unit which can take the whole group.

Role of "experts" and children's guardians

The views should be sought of therapists or other specialists who are already working with children on whether or not their needs are likely to be met by joint placement with siblings or not. It may also be useful to employ a social work expert, a psychologist or a child psychiatrist to contribute to an assessment of children's attachments to each other and to advise on joint or separate placements. Children's guardians (who operate in England, Wales and Northern Ireland but not in Scotland) also have an important role in representing each child and giving a view as to the best way of meeting their long-term needs. They will also provide an input on the child's own wishes and feelings and views, as expressed to them by the child.

However, it is very important that the local authority does not abdicate its own key responsibility for assessing and planning for the child and for ascertaining and taking account of his or her wishes, feelings and views. The child's foster carer and social worker should, and almost certainly do, know the child better than others who have met him or her on only a few occasions. The local authority workers need to be clear that, having listened to and taken note of the views of all the professionals involved, they must come to their own conclusion about what will be right for the child.

Permanency planning meetings

It can be very helpful to have a small team who meet regularly to make permanence plans for a child or sibling group. The group would include the children's social worker(s), foster carer(s) and a representative from the adoption and permanence team. Other professionals could make a contribution as necessary for particular children. The child's birth parents should also be involved if at all possible and if they are able to be helped to work constructively on planning for their child's future away from them. Members of this team would be involved in assessing the needs and wishes of children in a sibling group (see Chapter 5) and would reach a joint conclusion on the best plan. This should then be taken to a Review (specially convened if necessary) for formal confirmation.

Special siblings meeting

Some local authorities convene a special meeting, chaired either by a senior manager or by an independent reviewing officer, to consider and make decisions about either separating, uniting or re-uniting siblings in permanent placement. This emphasises the crucial importance of this decision. This should then be confirmed at a Review, which may need to be specially convened.

Reviews

Statutory child care reviews should be where important decisions about looked after children are considered and confirmed. We recommend that a Review, specially arranged if necessary, should make or confirm the final decision about permanently separating siblings.

It can be very helpful for one reviewing officer to review all looked after children in the same sibling group, whether these are birth siblings who are in separate placements or children growing up in the same permanent family who may not be related to each other. This enables there to be a clear overview of the sibling group(s) to which the child belongs. If siblings are being looked after by other local authorities, there will need to be liaison between workers.

It is essential that the review of each child includes information on siblings placed elsewhere and that their views and those of their carers have been sought if possible. The child's knowledge of siblings placed elsewhere and their wishes and feelings in relation to placement with these siblings or contact with them, should be sought, recorded, considered and discussed.

If children have siblings placed elsewhere and it is not possible to have one reviewing officer involved, care must be taken to link, in the review process, with those who are making decisions about the other children.

Panel

The adoption panel can make a useful contribution to decisions about the placement of siblings when it is considering plans for children. If it is an adoption and permanence panel, as an increasing number are, it can consider all the members of a sibling group even when some have fostering plans and others adoption plans. The panel does not have a statutory duty to recommend whether or not siblings should be separated. However, it can, of course, decline to recommend that adoption is right for a particular child if this will separate the child from siblings and if, in the panel's view, this is wrong. Panels can also make useful comments about whether siblings are likely to have their needs met if they remain together. They should ask about the assessment made of the sibling group as well as about siblings placed elsewhere and whether the possibility of a joint placement has been explored. When a panel considers a match, it is helpful if they can clarify whether there are any siblings placed elsewhere, still at home, or likely to be born and to need adoption and if they can check whether there has been any discussion with the new family about this and about the possibility of future contact or even placement.

There is useful guidance in *Effective Panels* (Lord and Cullen, 2006) for panel members when considering permanence as a plan for members of a sibling group.

The panel should consider each child as an individual in his or her own right as well as a member of a sibling group.

Panel members should also raise the following issues:

- *Who are the child's siblings?*

- *Why are siblings being placed separately if this is the proposed plan?*

- *Why are siblings, who may have very great and perhaps conflicting needs, being placed together if this is the proposed plan? It will be important to check whether siblings have been involved together in abusive situations and, if they have, whether they can break the abusive ways of relating that they have learned, as long as they remain together. Has appropriate work been undertaken with these children to facilitate change?*

- *How do the children get on with each other? The observations of their carers will be important and the agency may also have*

completed a sibling relationship checklist (see Appendix).

- *What are the wishes and feelings of the children themselves about being placed together or separately?*

- *If the children are currently living apart but the plan is for permanent placement together, what is being done to maintain or build a relationship between them?*

- *If the plan is for separate placements for siblings, what sort of contact between them is planned?*

- *What additional financial support may be available for a new family taking on a sibling group? Large sibling groups of five or six children can be found adoptive families but a package of financial support is often a vital factor in the viability of these placements.*

Decisions about contact

It is important to consider and make decisions about future contact at the same time as making decisions about possible separation of siblings. There should be a presumption that some form of contact will be beneficial unless there is clear evidence to the contrary. Issues around contact are discussed in Chapter 8.

Disruption of permanent placements

Sometimes, following the placement of a sibling group, the new family may feel unable to continue with the placement of one or more of the children but wish to continue to care for others.

Clearly there should be a programme of post-placement work and support offered to all families, and help provided if the family is experiencing particular difficulties with one child. However, in some situations this will not be enough. An assessment of how each child's needs are being met in the placement, work with each child to try and find out their wishes and feelings about a possible separation, and an assessment of the attachments between the siblings and of each child and the parents will need to be done before a decision is made to separate siblings in this situation. It may well be that the original assessment of the children underestimated the needs of a particular child and it now seems right to place him or her in another family and to support the remaining children in their current placement. However, it may be that the original family assessment overestimated their strengths and that the focus of difficulties will switch to another child if one is removed. Similar consideration needs to be given as to whether or not it is right to separate siblings at this stage as is given when deciding whether to remove some or all of a sibling group from birth parents or whether to separate them when planning a new permanent placement. This is a very important decision and should involve a group of people in the same way as the earlier decisions.

Whenever a separation does occur at this stage, it is essential that consideration is given to ongoing contact for the children.

5   Assessing children in sibling groups

It is important to do a full assessment of each individual child in a sibling group as well as an assessment of their relationships with each other and the dynamics of the group. Even if it seems clear that the siblings should remain together, a full assessment will provide essential information for a new family and will enable the agency to anticipate the extra help and support which will be necessary.

Clarify who the siblings are

It is important to clarify, at an early stage in planning, who the "core" sibling group includes who could be considered for a permanent placement together. In our case (Pg. 2) the three children needing permanent placement are Katie, David and Andrew. Andrew was removed from home as an infant and placed separately from Katie and David but it is important that careful consideration is given to uniting him with his older siblings.

Information needs to be gathered on other siblings living elsewhere, either with extended family or in foster or adoptive homes. At the very least, this information needs to be recorded, but the possibility of contact or even of placement together also needs to be carefully considered.

Each child needing a permanent placement needs an opportunity to say who they consider their brothers and sisters to be and who is important to them. However, there may well be siblings about whom they know nothing but who could be important to them.

Who should be involved?

Having established who the "core" group of siblings are for whom permanent plans need to be made, it is important that key people involved with the children are included in the assessment and planning process. Some agencies have "permanency planning meetings" which involve a team who meet regularly to plan for children. This team would include the social worker for each child, each foster carer if the children are placed separately, and a representative from the adoption and permanence team. Other people, such as a family centre staff member, who may be involved in joint contact sessions, or a psychologist or other therapist could also be included. Birth parents should also be included if they are able to be helped to participate in constructive planning for a new family for their children.

Children in separate foster homes

If siblings are currently placed in separate foster or residential homes, it is essential that they have opportunities to spend quality time together as a group. This could take place in a family centre or in one of the foster homes. However, it needs to be for more than an hour or two a week and it is important, if it takes place in a foster home, that other unrelated children are not routinely present. Siblings need an opportunity to build or rebuild a sense of themselves as a discrete group and those assessing their relationships need to see how the group functions without the distraction of other children.

Assessing each child's needs

When assessing and planning for a sibling group, it is very important to remember that each child is also an individual with his or her own unique needs. It is essential that each child in a sibling group has a full assessment in their own right. The assessment of their relationship with, and attachment to, their siblings is one component of this, but only one.

Assessment should start from the time of the first referral of a family to the social services or social work department. *The Assessment of Children in Need Framework* (DH, 2000) identifies clearly the components of this, i.e. health, education, emotional and behavioural development, identity, family and social relationships, social presentation and self-care skills.

These same components are the ones to be looked at and assessed in the Looking After Children Assessment and Action Record which most agencies now use for children whom they are looking after.

It is important to have the depth and range of information about each individual child, which these assessment formats require, when deciding whether the combined range of needs of the children in a sibling group could be met by one permanent family.

A child's relationship with siblings will be affected by the quality of the attachment each has had with their primary caregiver. There should be some assessment of this and a gathering of information on the attachment history of each child before the sibling relationship is considered.

What does each child understand and feel about what has happened so far and what are their wishes for the future?

It is important that each child in a sibling group has the opportunity for some individual sessions in which they can explore and reflect on their life at home, on the reasons why they are in care, and on what they would wish for in the future. This will include the opportunity for the child to express feelings about brothers and sisters, explore how much they identify with siblings, with whom they would like to live and with whom they would like more or less contact. The potential of disabled children to communicate their wishes, feelings and views is frequently underestimated but they may need extra help.

Each child in a sibling group should have their own life story book. However, useful work can be done with the siblings together and older children can be very helpful to younger ones in explaining what happened at home. A sibling group could usefully compile a family tree together, and talk about the significance of different family members. It is important to bear in mind, though, that some aspects of each child's experience of life at home will have been different and also that there may be family secrets which some or all of the children are trying to keep. There is a discussion of working with sibling groups, as well as with individual children, in *Life Story Work* (Ryan and Walker, 2007). If it is decided to split siblings and to place them separately, the reasons for this must be explained to

the child as fully and carefully as possible and should also be included in the child's life story book.

Context in which the relationship between siblings has developed

Many factors influence how siblings relate to each other and it is important to be aware of these when assessing the relationships between them. Some of these are usefully listed in *Patterns and Outcomes in Child Placement* (DH, 1991) and include:

- the children's position in the family;
- their gender;
- cultural and family expectations for each child;
- the emotional age at which each is functioning;
- the extent to which they have a shared history and family experience;
- the role each child is perceived to have played (if any) in the sibling group leaving home and starting to be looked after.

Another important factor is likely to be the child's innate temperament and degree of resilience.

Kosonen (1994) has written on factors in the birth family which can negatively influence the relationship between siblings. These include the following.

- Poor attachments to parents, which can result in intense sibling conflict.
- A conflictual relationship between parents can also result in poor sibling relationships, with a tendency for boys to be particularly affected.
- Parental favouritism is likely to increase sibling conflict and to be negative for both favoured and non-favoured children. However, if children can perceive differential treatment as "fair", their sibling relationships need not suffer.
- Neglect and parental unavailability can result in strong compensatory sibling relationships, particularly if an older sibling provides some parenting of younger children. However, in the absence of parental care and supervision, these sibling bonds may become abusive and/or result in unmet needs.
- Impact of abuse: This may result in poor and hostile sibling relationships for both abused and

non-abused children. Children who have been abused may be particularly resentful of those who have not.

- "High access" siblings, i.e. those close in age and of the same gender, can have an emotionally intense relationship with high levels of conflict.

- Impact of non-shared environment: It is important to remember that no two siblings will have exactly the same experience, either in their relationships with other family members or with those outside the family, such as other relatives, teachers, friends, etc. These individual factors can have an important effect on how each child relates to siblings.

Assessing a child's attachment to and relationship with each sibling

It is important, even in large sibling groups, to assess each child's relationship with every other child in the group. This assessment should be based on a detailed observation of how the children behave with each other. The observations of people who have seen the children together at different times and in different settings should be gathered. Current and previous foster carers, birth relatives, other siblings, teachers and social workers can all make useful observations, although it is important that these are backed up with concrete examples.

Sibling relationship checklists, reproduced from *Patterns and Outcomes in Child Placement* (HMSO, 1991), are included in an appendix to this practice guide.

Researchers (Furman and Buhrmester, 1985) have highlighted four key factors which need to be assessed in a sibling relationship. These are:

- the degree of warmth
- the degree of conflict
- the degree of rivalry
- the degree to which one of the siblings nurtures or dominates the other.

Dynamics of the sibling group

Having assessed the relationship of each pair of siblings it is then important, with large sibling groups, to look at the overall dynamics of the group. For instance, do two younger children get on fairly well together unless an older sibling is present, who winds them both up, leading to conflict? Does one child tend to be excluded or scapegoated by the others? Does one child appear to be doing the acting out on behalf of others? Does an older child appear to be very controlling of younger siblings? It should be kept in mind that, if one child is separated from the group, another child may take on their role and become, for example, the one who acts out.

Clearly, learned patterns of behaviour will have been brought from the birth family. If the children are currently in separate foster placements, they will also be starting to be affected by the dynamics of that family, and any particular factors in this should be noted. It can be helpful to collect any videos or DVDs of a sibling group before any plan is made to separate them. This can be a useful tool in assessment. It can, for instance, aid discussion of sibling interaction with a supervisor.

What work could be done to improve relationships between siblings?

The decision to separate permanently siblings who have lived or are currently living together should, in our view, be treated with the same seriousness as the decision to separate children permanently from their parents. For siblings, as for parent and child, an assessment of the relationship should be followed in most cases by a time-limited programme of work aimed at improving the relationship and preventing the need for a permanent separation.

There may be one child in a sibling group whose emotional and behavioural needs are so great that relationships with siblings are hostile and full of conflict. However, it is possible that some brief therapy for the particularly needy child, some direct work with each child, and some work with the group as a whole, could enable a joint placement to be made.

One adoptive family to whom we spoke described how their three older children had initially not wanted to be placed with their younger brother. When life story work was done it transpired that, when the children were still at home, this child had been taken out by his mother while the older three stayed at home and were abused by their stepfather.

When this was explored and talked through with the children, they could accept that this different treatment was beyond the control of them all and they became much less antagonistic to their brother and were eventually all placed together.

It is important that work with siblings, as with parents and children, is done in a planned way, with clear reviews and time-limits built in. It should, if possible, begin when work is being done with the birth family prior to children being looked after. Better relationships between siblings will be a major investment for their future, whether they remain within their birth family or have a permanent new family.

Circumstances which may indicate that siblings should be placed separately

There are a number of factors that may indicate the need for permanent separation. For example, very intense levels of conflict, dominant or abusive patterns of behaviour may mean that placement together is not viable. Careful consideration needs to take place for siblings who have been sexually abused as to whether they can be placed together permanently.

Burnell, Vaughan and Williams (2007), in their experience, state that children who have experienced very poor attachments need to develop a secure attachment to safe adult caregivers. Achieving this must take primary importance in care planning for the child. In their view, siblings who have been traumatised may need to be separated because, placed togther, they will inhibit the formation of this child to adult primary attachment.

Gerrilyn Smith, Clinical Psychologist, sets out a number of circumstances, indicated in the following six bullet points, which indicate that siblings may need to be placed separately. These are based on her extensive clinical experience (personal communication).

If children are placed in the same family, it may be impossible (within a reasonable timescale) to help them recover from dysfunctional and destructive patterns of interaction from the family of origin. These patterns include:

- intense rivalry and jealousy, with each child totally pre-occupied with, and unable to tolerate, the attention which their sibling(s) may be getting;

- exploitation, often based on gender, e.g. boys may have been seen (in their birth family) and see themselves as inherently superior to their sisters, with a right to dominate and exploit them;

- chronic scapegoating of one child; maintaining unhelpful alliances in a sibling group and family of origin conflicts – sibling patterns of behaviour may be strongly entrenched and may prevent re-parenting or learning new cultural norms;

- maintaining unhelpful hierarchical positions e.g. a child may be stuck in the role of victim or bully;

- highly sexualised behaviour with each other;

- acting as triggers to each other's traumatic material and potentially constantly re-traumatising each other. The triggers may well be unconscious, unintentional and mundane.

It should be noted that any of the above patterns and ways of relating may be transferred by a child into his or her new family even if separated from birth siblings and placed singly. New parents need to be made fully aware of these patterns of interaction, particularly if they are also parenting other children (see also Chapter 6).

There may be other reasons too.

- An older sibling may not be able to invest emotionally in a new family and will hinder the emotional investment of a younger child.

- There can be considerable age difference between siblings placed. Sometimes, the care plan for a much older sibling may be for permanent foster care with regular direct contact with birth family members but for a much younger sibling, adoption in a new family with indirect contact with the birth family is in their best interest.

- Sometimes a relative of one of the siblings offers a home to that child but not to others and this adult–child relationship is assessed as more important to the child than the sibling one.

- Sometimes a child may have a significant attachment to another carer and it is too damaging to disrupt this in order to unite or reunite the child with other siblings.

- Sometimes the size and age range of the group means that there are a very limited number of families available. After time-limited family finding, a sibling group may therefore need to be separated, but it is important that ongoing contact arrangements are made which can support the maintenance of their relationships.

For some children, the trauma of separation can be profound and the sense of loss may be longstanding. It is vitally important to record decisions and provide explanations to children as to why separation has occurred or will occur (Groze, 1996). Preparing children for such separations and supporting them and their families are vitally important tasks. Decisions about ongoing contact will need careful assessment.

Identifying who should be placed with whom if a sibling group needs to be split

As has been said elsewhere in this guide, separations which happen when children start to be looked after, often based purely on available foster care placements, can all too easily become permanent. An assessment of siblings' relationships with each other should start while they are still at home, and if removal from home seems likely, some thought should be given to possible future placement. If siblings may need to be separated in temporary foster placements, what is likely to work best? The level of need of individual children, the relationship between individual children and their own wishes will all be important factors. Several of the adoptive families to whom we spoke commented that, if children are very close in age, which they often are in large sibling groups, it can work best having taken into account the above factors, to consider placing children alternately, rather than in age order, i.e. the five and three-year-old together and the four and two-year-old together. This may reduce the intense rivalry and competition which there can be between

siblings who are very close in age, particularly if they are also of the same gender.

Separating children in permanent placement should only be contemplated following a full assessment of their needs, their wishes and their relationships, and this is likely to indicate who should be placed with whom, or whether they should be placed on their own. If the "ideal" is to place a large group together, efforts must be made first, albeit within agreed timescales, to recruit a family for the whole group. This is discussed in more detail in the next chapter. If children do have to be placed separately in this situation, and should family finding for the sibling group prove unsuccessful, the three key factors should again be:

- their individual needs;

- their wishes; and

- their relationships.

The same considerations are relevant to children who are very close in age, particularly if of the same gender, as discussed above. It will be essential to build in as much contact as possible for children separated because of a lack of resources. It will be important to try and recruit families who live fairly close to each other and who are committed to ongoing contact, probably involving having the whole group for some weekends and holiday periods.

Recording

It is very important that the reasons for deciding to separate siblings or to place them together are clearly recorded and evidenced. This record should include the children's own views and the reasons, where applicable, why it was decided to override these. This written information should be given to the new family, be included in each child's life story book and also be available on each child's adoption file held in the agency. When the children become adults, they may or may not feel that the right decision was made but they should at least be clear that it was made with thought and care, after a thorough assessment.

6 Recruiting, preparing and supporting new families

Issues around siblings will need to be discussed and addressed with virtually all prospective adopters and foster carers. They may be applying for a sibling group or they may be applying for a single child but have a child or children already in their family whose brother or sister the new child will become. They may already have several children and be applying for another sibling group. The child or children placed with them may well have siblings placed elsewhere and will need help to understand why this is and to maintain some contact with them if possible. Even if the family is childless and the child to be placed currently has no siblings, brothers or sisters may be born subsequently and adoptive families need to be prepared to receive news of this and to be asked, possibly, to be considered as parents to the second child too. They may well have a clear wish to apply for a second child at a later date, thus creating a sibling pair.

Time-limited foster families

There is a critical shortage of time-limited foster carers throughout the UK. This results in large numbers of sibling groups needing to be split and placed separately on entry to care. As discussed earlier, this can have disastrous consequences, leading sometimes to the permanent separation of brothers and sisters and in other cases making a joint permanent placement much harder to achieve.

A lot of the points made in the subsequent sections in relation to families offering permanence apply equally to time-limited foster carers. The need for families able to accommodate groups of three, four and more brothers and sisters needs to be made clear in all recruitment literature, in initial information meetings, and during preparation.

If families are able to take sibling groups of three or more, single children should not be placed with them if at all possible, although it is acknowledged that this may be very difficult when resources are so stretched. From the family's point of view, perhaps a retainer fee could be paid if there is a wait for a sibling group placement.

As with families offering permanence, additional support and practical help will probably be needed when families are caring for more than three children. (We do appreciate that, in many local authorities, many families are likely to have exemptions to care for more than three unrelated children placed at any one time.)

As has been discussed earlier, time-limited foster carers play a very important part in assessing the attachments and relationships between siblings and in listening to what the individual children in their care say about their siblings and what they would like for their future. It is helpful if they can keep a diary detailing the interaction of siblings placed with them. This may well change over time. Foster carers may need to work closely with other foster carers and a number of social workers to facilitate contact between siblings who are placed separately. These are all skilled tasks for which thorough preparation as well as good support will be needed.

Recruiting permanent new families

Families *can* be found for large sibling groups. Groups of four, five, six and even seven siblings have been successfully placed for adoption.

In the year to December 2007, 59 families were referred to the Adoption Register for England and Wales who were able to consider sibling groups of three children, and six who were able to consider groups of four children. Five groups of three siblings were placed via the Register in that year. In the year to March 2008, 10 groups of three children were placed as a result of being featured in *Be My Parent*, BAAF's monthly family-finding newspaper. One group of four children was placed in the same year. In total, 80 children in sibling groups were placed in that year. They received 731 enquiries from prospective families.

Some agencies have workers who concentrate on finding families for sibling groups. One voluntary agency has had time-limited project outreach workers to recruit, in turn, families for black children, families for disabled children and now, families for sibling groups.

However, inter-agency funding may well be needed and it will probably be necessary to publicise the need for families for sibling groups. If the plan is to try and find a family for a group of brothers and sisters together, it is likely to work best if they are photographed and profiled together, with a clear statement that they want and need to stay together. Only if it proves impossible to find a family for all the children within agreed timescales should the profile qualify this message and say that the agency would consider separating the children. A national survey by BAAF (Ivaldi, 2000) showed that, of the children adopted in 1998/9, almost all children for whom the plan was placement with siblings were, in fact, placed together. This included groups of four and five siblings.

None of the families to whom we spoke liked the term "sibling" or thought that it meant much to the general public. It is a convenient shorthand term but brothers and sisters means more to most people and is probably a more useful term to use in general publicity. As one adoptive parent commented, 'It seems much worse to separate brothers and sisters than to separate siblings!'

It is important for local authorities to be as clear as possible at the recruitment stage, whether this is general recruitment or for specific groups of children, about the support package which will be available. Potential adopters of large sibling groups may be put off altogether if they gather that support is not likely to be available. For some, adoption of more than one child will be impossible without practical and financial help. Others will choose to apply to an agency which does appear to take post-placement support seriously rather than to one which does not.

Preparing, assessing and approving families

The beliefs and views of the social workers doing assessments are inevitably factors in the process. They can influence decisions about whether siblings are placed together or separately, as discussed in Chapter 3, and they can also influence whether families are approved for large sibling groups or not. Family placement workers need opportunities for discussion and training about the placement of

siblings and an opportunity to discuss individual applications with team members as well as supervisors. A number of families to whom we spoke who were successfully parenting groups of four or more siblings, commented that they had had to convince family placement workers who tended to question how anyone could manage to take on more than two children at a time.

A number of families who have successfully adopted sibling groups of four or more were initially thinking of no more than two children. However, when social workers shared information on waiting children with them during the preparation process they were drawn to larger sibling groups. Families need to know that sibling groups are waiting and it is often useful to share information on all waiting children with individual families during the preparation process.

It is well known that families often say they learn most from talking with other families. Certainly a number of the families to whom we spoke had found it invaluable to be put in touch with other adopters of large sibling groups. If there are no such families known locally, Adoption UK offers a useful service to its members through its Experience Resource Bank of families with particular experiences. Through this, applicants can be put in touch with adopters who have taken large sibling groups, can talk on the phone and can arrange to visit and find out exactly what is involved.

It will be helpful to explore the applicants' own experience of siblings, both the sibling group, if any, in which they grew up and also sibling groups with whom they now have contact through their family and friendship networks. What are their expectations of how siblings relate to each other and are they prepared for the sibling rivalry and conflict to be considerably greater than usual for children whose parenting has been inadequate and disrupted? Families need to be prepared for the fact that many siblings to be placed as a group are living in separate foster families and may have limited experience or even no experience, of living together. On the other hand, some sibling groups may have very close bonds, which could feel quite excluding to new parents. It may emerge in placement that the children have been involved in sexually abusive relationships with each other and families need to be prepared for this.

It is important that the positives of parenting a sibling group are also discussed during the assessment and preparation period. Brothers and sisters can be very supportive to each other and several of the families to whom we spoke commented that their children played well together and kept each other entertained and occupied. Siblings also have a shared history and can support each other and help each other remember and deal with their feelings about what happened at home.

If the prospective adopters already have children, it is clearly important for them to be fully involved in the preparation process. Research (Rushton *et al*, 2001) indicates that the experience of being a sibling already may be useful preparation. However, it also demonstrates that even grown up children who have left home can still experience jealousy and need to be involved in the initial preparation. It is important to remember that siblings being placed may bring dysfunctional patterns of relating and behaving into the new family. Children already in the family risk getting involved in these patterns. A child who has been separated from siblings and placed singly may also attempt to relate to any new children in the family as he or she did with birth siblings e.g. take on the scapegoat or victim role or attempt to bully or dominate.

Support after placement will be essential, and is discussed in more detail in the next section. Agencies need to explore with families during the assessment and preparation stage what their own support networks will be and also to be clear about what support the agency will be able to offer. It is important for new parents to be able to spend some time with each child individually and they will need to think about how they will manage this.

Adoption panel members can sometimes be very cautious about approving applicants, particularly childless people, for more than two children. Obviously each case must be considered very carefully on its own merits. However, it is important that panel members are aware that childless applicants, and those with children, have successfully adopted large sibling groups of four or more children. Several of the families to whom we spoke thought that their attendance at panel to present themselves and to answer questions directly, had been crucial to their approval for a large sibling group.

A national survey by BAAF (Ivaldi, 2000) showed that over 50 per cent of adopters who were prepared to consider two children, had single children placed with them. Of adopters prepared to consider three children, 20 per cent had single children placed and 33 per cent had two children placed.

Supporting families

Good support packages for families are absolutely essential if they are to parent large sibling groups.

- **Financial support** is almost certain to be needed. They can be paid (subject to the required means test) when siblings are being placed together and also when a single child is joining siblings who are already placed.

- **A settling-in grant** for equipment such as beds, larger washing machine, etc. will also probably be needed.

- **Domestic help** could be provided in the early stages of a placement.

- **Transport** is an issue and a family who will have more than three children (including any they already have) will need a larger than average car, for which financial help may be necessary.

- **Housing** will be an issue for some families. Some local authorities have made a loan or grant to enable an extension to be built or to enable a house move. The legal department in one agency wrote to the family's building society, guaranteeing that their income, which consisted largely of adoption allowances, would not fall below the current level for x years, thus enabling the building society to make a loan. Another local authority made a loan to a family enabling an extension to be built. An agreement was drawn up stating that it need not be re-paid provided the children were still in placement after 10 years. These arrangements need careful thought and planning and it is vital that they are not left to the last minute. With the help of the legal department, it should be possible to make an arrangement which can be changed should, for instance, a placement disrupt.

- **Therapeutic help** may also be needed and this too needs to be thought about and planned. For one family a package of help and support was set up with the local Children and Adolescent Mental

Health Service (CAMHS). The adopters have monthly consultation sessions which help them to support and work with their children. Should the children need individual or group therapy, there is a guarantee that this will be offered. Another family has funding agreed and access to art and music therapy for three of their children.

- **Specific help and support** may be needed for the new family on working with the children's relationship with each other. This may involve the placed sibling group and also any existing children in the family and their relationship with the placed children. Research (Rushton *et al*, 2001) indicates that sibling relationship difficulties are a factor in less stable placements and that it is crucial that appropriate support and funding for specialist help are available if necessary.

7 Timing of introductions and placement

Sometimes children who currently live together are to be placed separately in new permanent families. In other situations, children who are currently in separate placements are to be re-united or united into a permanent new family. In each case, careful thought needs to be given to how to prepare children and families, and how to manage introductions and placement. The logistics of preparing a new family for the placement of a large sibling group of perhaps four or more children, and managing introductions, even if the children are in the same temporary placement, also needs careful planning.

It can be very helpful to have a Life Appreciation Day before introductions start. This is an opportunity for important adults in the children's lives, their parents and other important relatives if possible, their foster carers, both past and present, their teachers, etc. to meet with the prospective new parents to talk about the children. These meetings need careful preparation and good facilitation and they complement rather than take the place of individual meetings and written information. However, they can give a very rich, full and "living" picture of children.

There is a more detailed discussion of the issues which need to be considered when linking and introducing children and new families in BAAF's Practice Guide, *Linking and Introductions* (Byrne, 2000).

Logistics of placing a large group, currently living together, into the same permanent family

It is vital that enough time is built into the process for new parents to learn about each child as an individual, prior to meeting them, as well as about the dynamics of the group. The family needs the opportunity to read about, talk about and think about each child as they would if they were considering a single child. Each child will have his or her own history and own unique experience of family life. He or she will have their own particular needs and time must be taken, for instance, to meet therapists, doctors, teachers or others who can contribute

information on the individual child. The child's current carers will have invaluable information to give and it may well be that several meetings rather than the usual one are needed before the new family meet the children, to talk with the foster carers about each individual child as well as about how they function as a group in the context of this particular foster family.

The new parents should probably meet all the children together on the first occasion. However, opportunities should be built into the introductory process to spend time with each child individually as well. Introductions are always tiring and quite stressful but are likely to be even more so when a number of children are involved at the same time. It is vital that support is available from the agency in practical ways – e.g. help with transport – and also that time is made available for discussion and reflection.

It will probably be best in most situations to place the children at the same time. However, it could be agreed that the placements are staggered. Vera Fahlberg (1994) suggests that it can be helpful to place the oldest child, or the one likely to take the most time and energy, first, when the new parents' energy levels are highest. In a sibling group which includes a disabled child, it might be a good idea for that child to be placed and settled first. When an older child has parented younger siblings, he or she could be placed first, to build a rapport with the parents and to then help introduce the younger siblings when appropriate.

Children currently placed together who are to go to separate permanent families

Clearly any decision to place children separately who are currently together should be based on a careful and thorough assessment of their needs and their relationship, and should involve the children as well as the current carers.

Children and carers will also need to be involved in discussion about what happens next and about the family finding process. It could be, for example, that a younger child is going to be placed for adoption as soon as possible while an older child is to have a period of work or therapy prior to moving on. The children will need to be prepared for what is to happen so that, as far as possible, the older child can understand why he or she has been left behind while ensuring that the younger child doesn't feel pushed out or rejected.

When family finding is being done simultaneously for individual children, they and their carers will need help and support to accept that chance will play some part in whose family is identified first. However, it will also be important to be honest with children and, for example, to tell them that not so many families are able to look after older children.

If the current foster carers are not in agreement with the plan to place the children separately, or if the relationship between the children is harmful because they are abusing each other or are very aggressive, it may be best to use another bridging foster home and to place one or both of the children in a new placement on their own prior to their permanent placement. While any move for a child is critical and should be carefully thought about and planned, it may be, in the above situations, that it is helpful for the child to have a short period living apart from their sibling before being introduced to a permanent new family. Introductions are also likely to be much easier and more productive if the foster carer is able to help the child move on in a positive way.

Children currently in separate placements who are to be re-united or united in a permanent placement

An essential first stage in this process is for the children to have frequent contact as a sibling group. Foster carers need to be involved in this and ideally will each have experienced having the whole group for a period, as well as meeting together. It is important for the sibling group to have had an opportunity for periods of time together, without other foster children or birth children of foster carers present. Social workers will almost certainly need to be involved in this, as well as foster carers, and the aim should be for the children to spend as much time as possible together in periods of a day or half a day at a time, ideally several times a week. They may well need to "practise" being together and it is

helpful if they can have built or re-built their relationships with each other, to some extent at least, before embarking on a permanent placement together.

As well as talking with the social workers for the children, reading about each child, meeting specialists involved with each child, etc., the new parents need to talk individually with each foster family to learn about the individual children and the dynamics of the child or children with each other and with other children in that foster family. It may also be helpful to have an opportunity to meet with the various foster carers together, to hear their comments on the whole sibling group. Some of the complexities involved are illustrated below.

Lisa, aged six, and Angelina, aged four, are placed with foster carers Anne and Mike. Anne and Mike have birth daughters of nine and 11. Lisa and Angelina's younger brother, Paul, aged three, is placed with a single carer, Sue, who has a son of eight. Lisa's, Angelina's and Paul's infant brother, Joshua, is placed with an older couple, Connie and Jim. The children are of white English and Irish parentage.

Connie and Jim think that Joshua should be placed on his own. They haven't had the care of all four siblings as they don't think that they could cope. They think the four children will be too much for any family.

Sue has taken Paul to see his brother and sisters when they've all met up at a family centre. She is committed to them being placed together but can't quite believe that any one family will cope. She hasn't had care of all four children together. Paul is close to her son of eight and she knows the two boys will miss each other.

Anne and Mike are the only foster family of the three who have cared for all four siblings together. They are used to caring for four children – their own two daughters and two foster children – and are very positive about the four siblings being placed together. Anne and Mike have seen how Lisa and Angelina look up to their daughters and then, in turn, mother their own two brothers. They have observed how Paul is quite wary of Mike, having been abused by his own father and currently living with a single female foster carer. Anne and Mike make time to

Family tree

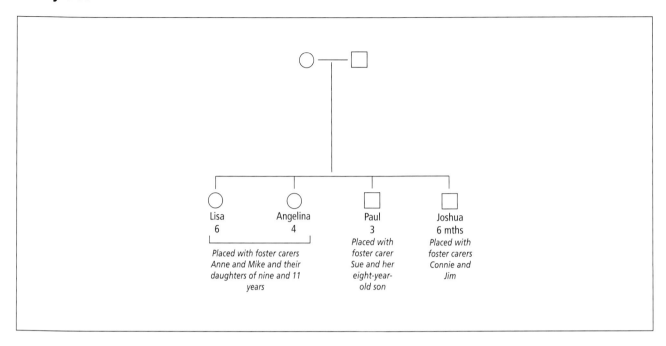

Placed with foster carers Anne and Mike and their daughters of nine and 11 years

Lisa 6 — Angelina 4

Paul 3 — *Placed with foster carer Sue and her eight-year-old son*

Joshua 6 mths — *Placed with foster carers Connie and Jim*

have Lisa, Angelina, Paul and Joshua together in their home when their own daughters are out, to give the four siblings a chance to experience being together in a family home.

New parents will need to spend time individually with each foster family to learn about the individual children and the sibling group and to get a feel of the different foster family each child has been used to. They may be experiencing different parenting styles and different family lifestyles. Some foster carers, like Anne and Mike in our example, will also be able to talk more about how the children are together.

Having met all the foster families, the adopters will need to meet the children together, as well as seeing them in their own foster homes. In our example, it

may well be helpful, after a period of introductions, to have Lisa and Angelina placed first, before settling in Paul and then Joshua. A gap of just a week or two between placements can be helpful, although some families find that a month or two to settle in an older child before younger ones join the family can work well. The age of the children and their own wishes will be important factors in this, as will be the views and wishes of the new family.

Burnell, Vaughan and Williams (2007) suggest that, in their view, an introduction and settling-in period of six to nine months may be helpful before a second child is introduced. They comment that this will enable the parent to feel 'confident and comfortable' in their relationship with the first sibling and able, then, to focus on the needs of the second sibling.

8 Post-placement contact

Introduction

Sometimes decisions are made to place children separately from at least some of their brothers and sisters. Other siblings may also already be permanently placed elsewhere or may be adult and it is not possible or advisable to reunite or to unite them. However, wherever children are placed apart from siblings, consideration should always be given to the possibility of some form of contact between them. Some children may not want contact early on in their placement but may change their mind when they feel more secure. Agencies should always be prepared to negotiate or renegotiate sibling contact if this is requested. For siblings who have tenuous relationships and live apart, ongoing and meaningful contact can be an investment for the future when relationships could become significant and enduring over time. We do not yet know the outcomes for children of contact between siblings over the long term. More research is needed. However, they would seem promising, given studies to date. The opportunity to know and, wherever possible, to be encouraged to develop positive and enduring relationships with brothers and sisters is a highly important one.

Information should be gathered on siblings as part of the initial work, as detailed in the *Assessment of Children in Need Framework* (DH, 2000), as soon as a family becomes known to social services. It should certainly be sought out and information put in writing on the child's file once the child starts being looked after. Contact should be made with the families with whom siblings are living, if at all possible, and once adoption or permanent fostering becomes the plan, consideration should be given to what contact, if any, would be beneficial to the child. This is then an important factor which needs to be taken into consideration when a new family is sought.

It will be important to clarify the purpose of continued contact arrangements between separated siblings and whether these arrangements will be beneficial for the children concerned. Burnell, Vaughan and Williams (2007) suggest a number of factors that should be considered in assessing sibling contact arrangements. These include: assessment of each child's individual development; consideration of the nature of the current sibling relationship; consideration of innate factors in each child, such as global developmental delay; and being clear as to the purpose of contact. The involvement of carers and parent, venue, supervision and frequency all need to be fully addressed and agreed. Furthermore, children's views need to be considered and any risks to safety and loss of confidentiality fully assessed and clarified. Issues around the behaviour and capacity of birth parents, adult birth relatives as well as foster carers and adopters to support the contact for children will also need consideration.

Contact may be face-to-face, by phone, or it may be indirect, in the form of letters and cards. It may be facilitated between the families concerned or social work help may be needed. There will certainly need to be social work involvement initially, to introduce families and to help them sort out an agreement about arrangements for contact. If there is a large sibling group who are split, it may be helpful, or even necessary, to have some or all of the contacts in twosomes rather than all together. However, it will be necessary to consider the number and frequency of different contact arrangements in relation to what children and their new parents can realistically accommodate in their new life together.

Macaskill (2002) undertook a study of older children placed for adoption or permanent fostering, all of whom had suffered emotional trauma. She found that, for a number of the children who had experienced abuse within the birth family, patterns of dominance, continuing anger at separation or sexual exploitation could resurface during contact meetings between siblings. She also found that some children wanted less contact as their relationship became more secure in their new family. They wanted to move on from the past whereas another sibling did not or could not.

The deciding factor regarding contact between siblings always has to be the needs of individual children. Like the decision to separate siblings, there may be a number of compelling reasons indicating that there should be no direct or even indirect contact in particular cases. This will need to be based on a careful assessment of the children's needs and wishes and on the family history. It could be that the child is clear that they wish to have no contact at all, at least for the time being. It could be that the relationship between the siblings is an abusive one and any form of contact is likely to result in extreme distress, continuing trauma or a return to previous dsyfunctional patterns of behaviour. It could be that a birth parent poses a serious threat to the child's permanent placement and so it is not possible for the child to have direct contact with siblings who remain living with the birth family (Bond, 2007).

Macaskill also found there were situations where contact worked well between siblings who had experienced abuse and trauma. There was good interaction, affection and it enabled siblings to talk about their past traumas helpfully together.

Contact for children in different adoptive families

Research (Lowe *et al*, 1999, Rushton *et al*, 2001, Smith and Logan, 2004) indicates that adoptive families are, on the whole, very open to facilitating contacts with siblings placed in other adoptive families. As well as seeing it as important for the children, adopters often value the contact as a source of support for themselves. Some families are able to establish friendly relationships with the families caring for their children's siblings who become members of the extended family, particularly if the families are not too geographically dispersed and if the adults have been able to form some sort of relationship. It is important that consideration is given, when looking at potential families for a child, to where their separated siblings are placed and to how contact between them can best be ensured.

Agencies should consider setting up a meeting between the families of separated siblings and helping them draw up a plan for contact. This may well be direct contact, ideally enabling the children to spend "quality" time together, including staying overnight in each others' homes and sharing some holidays together. The families will need to discuss the children's behaviour and routines. They will need to be clear why the children were placed separately and whether there are safety issues to be managed. Other children in each family, either birth children or adopted, will need to be carefully prepared and involved.

Other forms of contact can also be very helpful either instead of, or in addition to, direct contact e.g. the exchange of birthday cards and holiday postcards, letters, e-mails and phone calls. These could either be sent directly between the two families or could, if necessary, be arranged through the agency's letterbox scheme. Home movies can also be a very useful way of keeping memories alive between infrequent direct contacts, particularly for young children. It can be especially helpful to film part of the direct contact and to show this as a reminder, e.g. 'Do you remember when we had a picnic with Lee? Here you both are eating chocolate cake.' Videos or DVD films can also be valuable in some cases when it has been decided that there should be no face-to-face contact.

It is important that the families have access to an adoption support service, so that changes in contact or issues which arise, can be discussed. It can happen that one adoptive family stops contact and the agency should be prepared to try and mediate in this situation.

Contact with siblings in foster families

This contact can work in the same way as that between adoptive families. However, a difference is that children who are fostered are perhaps more likely to be in direct contact with birth relatives and this may raise safety and confidentiality concerns for adoptive families. It will probably be helpful for the local authority to arrange a meeting with the foster carers and the adopters so that there can be joint discussion and an agreement drawn up about the contact that the siblings will have with each other.

Difficulties can arise when the child in the new permanent family previously lived with brothers and sisters who have remained in the foster home. This may be the case if the child left because the placement disrupted or if the foster carers had wanted to keep the child but the child was moved on to an adoptive family. Care will need to be taken by the agency to negotiate contact arrangements and to rebuild bridges with the foster carers.

It is important to note that sometimes adopted children may worry about their siblings, placed elsewhere, particularly if they are not settled with a permanent family. In Smith and Logan's (2004) study of contact in adoption, they found that adopters expressed concerns about contact with siblings who remained looked after. They were worried about the impact of the looked after siblings' sexual knowledge and experience, their language, and rough and excitable behaviour when they met their adopted siblings. Those adopters felt contact was not an easy option but considered it to be very important, particularly for the siblings who remained looked after.

Contact with children still with parents or with other relatives

Research (Lowe et al, 1999) suggests that adopted children often want contact with siblings living with the birth family to satisfy themselves that their siblings are safe. Where this contact happens at all, it is usually as a side effect of the child having contact with the adults caring for their sibling. However, consideration should be given to the benefit for the children of having contact with each other in their own right. Clearly, the views and attitudes of the birth relatives will be crucial. However, with some work and support it might be possible for a birth parent or other relative to agree to siblings having some form of contact with each other, separately from themselves. This will almost certainly involve social work input to facilitate letterbox contact or to provide transport for visits. Clearly, safety and confidentiality issues will need to be carefully considered. It is important to recognise that levels of confidentiality may not be possible to maintain. Children should not be expected to keep secrets from one another and cannot be expected to differentiate between what will and will not be an identifying factor for birth relatives. Workers will need to support adopters and foster carers to accept this and think through any possible consequences, should direct contact be arranged.

Differing contact needs and/or arrangements for children placed together

Children growing up together in a permanent new family as brothers and sisters may or may not have the same birth family. Even if they do, they may have different contact needs and wishes. This was highlighted as a potentially problematic issue in a study of post-adoption contact:

> *Attempting to meet the respective needs of the children for contact could cause conflict and introduce severe stresses and strains for the adopters.* (DH, 1995)

Differing contact needs should not usually be a reason for placing children separately. However, it is vital to assess and be clear about each child's contact needs before placement, to discuss these with the children, with the birth relatives (including siblings placed elsewhere), and with prospective adopters. It may be that compromises will need to be negotiated and agreed. For instance, it might be agreed that an older child would, initially at least, have letterbox rather than face-to-face contact with his or her mother to ensure the safety and confidentiality of a younger half-sibling placed with him or her, whose birth father, currently living with the mother, would pose a considerable threat to the younger child.

Ongoing social work help and support may well be needed to manage these contacts and to review and change them as necessary, to take account of the children's changing needs.

> *John, aged eight, is to be placed for adoption with his infant half-brother Adam. The boys' mother, Linda, would like face-to-face contact with John, but not with Adam, with whom she never bonded. John would also like to see his mother occasionally. However, Adam's father, who still lives with Linda, is a schedule 1 offender and has threatened to seek Adam out if he can. It is agreed that John will have letterbox contact rather than direct contact with his mother, to ensure that he isn't pressured into revealing Adam's whereabouts. John is helped to understand this. He is very protective of Adam and wants to live with him, even though he knows that this means that he won't see his mother. John also has letterbox contact with his paternal grandparents.*

Siblings born subsequently or changes in circumstances for siblings

There should always be discussion with families taking a child on a permanent basis about arrangements for notifying them should a sibling of their child be born or start being looked after. It can be helpful if a brief written agreement is drawn up in which the family and the agency agree for this information, plus other changes in the birth family, e.g. the death of a parent, to be passed on. At the very least, the child in placement then has information about the existence of a sibling. Consideration can also be given as to the viability of some form of contact and to the possibility of the new child joining their brother or sister in the placement.

9 Conclusion

Brothers and sisters have potentially the longest lasting and one of the closest relationships of their lives with each other. Children need to be thought of in relation to their brothers and sisters, as well as in relation to their parents and carers, from the point of their referral to children's services/social work departments. In this guide, we have concentrated on children for whom a new permanent placement is the plan. However, as we have indicated, vital decisions are often made at a much earlier stage which will affect whether or not brothers and sisters grow up together or separately.

Key issues

There are a number of key issues already identified and discussed earlier which need addressing in relation to children in need as well as to looked after children for whom a permanent new placement may be the plan. These are summarised below.

- **Who are the child's brothers and sisters?** This will involve talking to each child and to their parents and other birth relatives, as well as reading any files which may already exist for the family. Information gathered should be clearly recorded. (Chapter 1)

- **What about siblings living elsewhere?** Consideration needs to be given not only to the sibling group who may be living together but also to whether children could be united or re-united with brothers and sisters living elsewhere. (Chapter 3)

- **What if siblings need to be separated?** If children need to be separated when they start being looked after purely because of a lack of placements, careful consideration should be given to who is placed with whom, regular contact should be arranged, and consideration should be given to re-uniting the children as soon as possible. (Chapters 3 and 4)

- **What are the child's assessed needs?** A full assessment should be done. (Chapter 5)

- **What is the child's relationship with each of his or her brothers and sisters?** (Chapter 5 and Appendix – Sibling Relationship Checklist)

- **What are the child's wishes and feelings** in relation to living permanently with or having contact with each of his or her brothers and sisters? (Chapter 5)

- **Could more work or resources help prevent children being or remaining permanently separated** from their brothers and sisters? (Chapters 3 and 5)

- **Are there valid reasons for keeping separated brothers and sisters apart** or for placing them separately if they currently live together? (Chapters 3 and 5)

- **How and by whom will this decision be made?** (Chapter 4)

- **If brothers and sisters are to be placed separately, the reasons for this should be clearly recorded.** (Chapter 5)

- **Introductions and placement:** Careful consideration needs to be given to the timing and logistics of introductions and placement, particularly if children are being separated or united. (Chapter 7)

- **Contact needs:** If brothers and sisters are to be placed separately or to remain in separate placements, their need for contact with each other should be carefully considered and a contact plan recorded. It should be clear how and when this will be reviewed. (Chapter 8)

- **Support needs:** It is essential that the post-placement and post-adoption support needs of new families who may be parenting sibling groups are recognised and addressed. (Chapter 6)

References

BAAF (2000) *Linking Children with Adoptive Families*, London: BAAF

Bank, S and Kahn, M (1982) *The Sibling Bond*, New York: Basic Books

Becket, C, Groothues, C and O'Connor, G (1999) 'The role of sibling group structure in adoption outcomes', in Mullender A (ed) *We are Family: Sibling relationships in placement and beyond*, London: BAAF

Bond (2007) *Ten Top Tips for Managing Contact*, London: BAAF

Burnell, A, Vaughan, J and Williams, L (2007) *Family Futures Assessment Handbook: Framework for assessing children who have experienced developmental trauma*, London: Family Futures

Byrne, S (2000) *Linking and Introductions: Helping children join adoptive families*, London: BAAF

Department of Health (1990) *The Care of Children. Principles and Practice in Regulations and Guidance*, London: HMSO

Department of Health (1991) *Patterns and Outcomes in Child Placement: Messages from current research and their implications*, London: HMSO

Department of Health (1995) *Moving Goalposts: A study of post-adoption contact in the north of England*, London: HMSO

Department of Health (1995) *Looking After Children: Assessment and Action Record*, London: HMSO

Department of Health (1999) *Adoption: Achieving the right balance*, London: HMSO

Department of Health, Department for Education and Employment, Home Office (2000) *Framework for the Assessment of Children in Need and their Families*, London: The Stationery Office

Elgar, M and Head, A (1997) *From Court Process to Care Plan: An empirical study of the placement of sexually abused children*, Oxford: The Centre for Socio-Legal Studies, Wolfson College, Oxford University

Fahlberg, V (1994) *A Child's Journey through Placement*, London: BAAF

Farmer, E and Pollock, S (1998) *Sexually Abused and Abusing Children in Substitute Care*, Chichester: John Wiley and Sons

Furman, W and Buhrmester, D (1985) 'Children's perceptions of the qualities of sibling relationships', *Child Development* 56

Groze (1996) *Successful Adoptive Families: A longitudinal study of special needs adoption*, New York: Praegar

Hegar (2005) 'Sibling placement in foster care and adoption: an overview of international research', *Children and Youth Services Review*, 27.7, pp717–739

Ivaldi, G (2000) *Surveying Adoption: A comprehensive analysis of local authority adoptions 1998-1999, England*, London: BAAF

Kosonen, M (1994) 'Sibling relationships for children in the care system', *Adoption and Fostering*: 18(3)

Kosonen, M (1996) 'Maintaining sibling relationships: neglected dimension in child care practice', *British Journal of Social Work*, 26

Kosonen, M (1999) ' "Core" and "kin" siblings: foster children's changing families' in Mullender, A (ed) *We are Family*, London: BAAF

Lord, J and Cullen, D (2006) *Effective Panels* (3rd edition), London: BAAF

Lowe, N, Murch, M, Borkowski, M, Weaver, A, Beckford, V and Thomas, C (1999) *Supporting Adoption: Reframing the Approach*, London: BAAF

Macaskill, C (1991) *Adopting or Fostering a Sexually Abused Child*, London: Batsford

Macaskill, C (2002) *Safe Contact? Children in permanent placement and contact with their birth relatives*, London: Russell House Publishing

Mullender, A (ed) (1999) *We are Family: Sibling relationships in placement and beyond*, London: BAAF

Neil, E (1999) 'The sibling relationships of adopted children and patterns of contact after adoption' in Mullender, A (ed) *We are Family*, London: BAAF

Parker, B A (1966) *Decisions in Child Care*, London: Allen and Unwin

Prevatt Goldstein, B (1999) 'Black siblings: a relationship for life' in Mullender, A (ed) *We are Family*, London: BAAF

Prevatt Goldstein, B and Spencer, M (2000) *'Race' and Ethnicity: A consideration of issues for black, minority ethnic and white children in family placement*, London: BAAF

Quinton, D, Rushton, A, Dance, C and Mayes, D (1998) *Joining New Families: Establishing permanent placements in middle childhood*, Chichester: John Wiley and Sons

Rushton, A, Treseder, J and Quinton, D (1989) 'Sibling groups in permanent placements', *Adoption and Fostering* 4, BAAF

Rushton, A, Dance, C, Quinton, D and Mayes, D (2001) *Siblings in Late Permanent Placements*, London: BAAF

Ryan, T and Walker, R (2007) *Life Story Work* (3rd edition), London: BAAF

Smith, C and Logan, J (2004) *After Adoption: Direct contact and relationships*, London: Routledge

Wedge, P and Mantle, G (1991) *Sibling Groups and Social Work: A study of children referred for permanent substitute family placement*, Aldershot: Avebury

Useful addresses

Adoption UK
46 The Green, South Bar Street
Banbury
Oxfordshire OX16 9AB
Tel: 01295 752240
www.adoptionuk.org
Supporting adoptive families before, during and after adoption

BAAF
Head Office
Saffron House, 6–10 Kirby Street
London EC1N 8TS
Tel: 020 7421 2600 (switchboard)
www.baaf.org.uk

Cymru
7 Cleeve House, Lambourne Crescent
Cardiff CF14 5GP
Tel: 029 2076 1155

Scotland
40 Shandwick Place
Edinburgh EH2 4RT
Tel: 0131 220 4749

Northern Ireland
Botanic House
1–5 Botanic Avenue
Belfast BT7 1JG
Tel: 028 9031 5494

Fostering Network
87 Blackfriars Road
London SE1 8HA
Tel: 020 7620 6400
www.fostering.net

Sibling relationships – checklists

The following checklists were included in *Patterns and Outcomes in Child Placement*, produced by the Department of Health in their series *The Children Act 1989* and published by HMSO in 1991. They were based on material from The Bridge Child Care Consultancy Service. This Crown copyright material is reproduced with the permission of The Controller of Her Majesty's Stationery Office.

The checklists are tools for observing and describing in concrete terms the way siblings relate to each other. They should form part of the evidence on which a decision about the placement of siblings is made but should not be the only evidence used.

The checklists must be completed by people who know the children and who can observe their behaviour at first hand. It can be helpful if they are completed by different people, observing the children in different settings, and the findings compared.

All three parts of the checklist must be completed for each sibling pair.

It is important that the completed checklists are analysed by a group. The group should identify positive and negative behaviours for each pair, but should remember that both are present in all sibling relationships. According to those who devised and first used the checklists, some types of behaviour seem to have particular significance in relation to the quality of a relationship. These are:

- sharing in boisterous play;

- resolving conflict through age-appropriate reasoning;

- reciprocal attempts to alleviate distress.

It is important that the context in which the relationship has developed is borne in mind when interpreting the information gathered. This is described more fully in Chapter 5.

The contents of the checklists that follow have been reproduced faithfully; however, we have asked, in addition, for the name of the person completing the checklist as well as their relationship to the child.

SIBLING RELATIONSHIP CHECKLIST 1

Child A _____ DOB _____

Child B _____ DOB _____

Behaviour of Child A to Child B   *Frequency (select one)*

A Defends or protects   1 Often ☐   2 Sometimes ☐   3 Never ☐

Examples of this behaviour _____

_____

B Recognises sib's distress and offers comfort   1 Often ☐   2 Sometimes ☐   3 Never ☐

Examples of this behaviour _____

_____

C Accepts comfort from sib   1 Often ☐   2 Sometimes ☐   3 Never ☐

Examples of this behaviour _____

_____

D Teaches or helps   1 Often ☐   2 Sometimes ☐   3 Never ☐

Examples of this behaviour _____

_____

E Initiates play   1 Often ☐   2 Sometimes ☐   3 Never ☐

Examples of this behaviour _____

_____

F Responds to overtures to play   1 Often ☐   2 Sometimes ☐   3 Never ☐

Examples of this behaviour _____

_____

G   Openly shows affection   1 Often ☐   2 Sometimes ☐   3 Never ☐

Examples of this behaviour _____

_____

H   Misses sib when apart   1 Often ☐   2 Sometimes ☐   3 Never ☐

Examples of this behaviour _____

_____

I   Resolves conflict through age-appropriate reasoning   1 Often ☐   2 Sometimes ☐   3 Never ☐

Examples of this behaviour _____

_____

J   Annoys, irritates or teases   1 Often ☐   2 Sometimes ☐   3 Never ☐

Examples of this behaviour _____

_____

K   Shows hostility or aggression   1 Often ☐   2 Sometimes ☐   3 Never ☐

Examples of this behaviour _____

_____

L   Blames or attempts to get sib into trouble   1 Often ☐   2 Sometimes ☐   3 Never ☐

Examples of this behaviour _____

_____

M   Behaviour sabotages efforts to meet other sib's needs   1 Often ☐   2 Sometimes ☐   3 Never ☐

Examples of this behaviour _____

_____

SIBLING RELATIONSHIP CHECKLIST 2

Child B _____   DOB _____

Child A _____   DOB _____

Behaviour of Child B to Child A   *Frequency (select one)*

A Defends or protects   1 Often ☐   2 Sometimes ☐   3 Never ☐

Examples of this behaviour _____

_____

B Recognises sib's distress and offers comfort   1 Often ☐   2 Sometimes ☐   3 Never ☐

Examples of this behaviour _____

_____

C Accepts comfort from sib   1 Often ☐   2 Sometimes ☐   3 Never ☐

Examples of this behaviour _____

_____

D Teaches or helps   1 Often ☐   2 Sometimes ☐   3 Never ☐

Examples of this behaviour _____

_____

E Initiates play   1 Often ☐   2 Sometimes ☐   3 Never ☐

Examples of this behaviour _____

_____

F Responds to overtures to play   1 Often ☐   2 Sometimes ☐   3 Never ☐

Examples of this behaviour _____

_____

G Openly shows affection   1 Often ☐   2 Sometimes ☐   3 Never ☐

Examples of this behaviour _____

_____

H Misses sib when apart   1 Often ☐   2 Sometimes ☐   3 Never ☐

Examples of this behaviour _____

_____

I Resolves conflict through age-appropriate reasoning   1 Often ☐   2 Sometimes ☐   3 Never ☐

Examples of this behaviour _____

_____

J Annoys, irritates or teases   1 Often ☐   2 Sometimes ☐   3 Never ☐

Examples of this behaviour _____

_____

K Shows hostility or aggression   1 Often ☐   2 Sometimes ☐   3 Never ☐

Examples of this behaviour _____

_____

L Blames or attempts to get sib into trouble   1 Often ☐   2 Sometimes ☐   3 Never ☐

Examples of this behaviour _____

_____

M Behaviour sabotages efforts to meet other sib's needs   1 Often ☐   2 Sometimes ☐   3 Never ☐

Examples of this behaviour _____

_____

SIBLING RELATIONSHIP CHECKLIST 3

Interactions

1 What evidence is there of sharing:

Examples

Boisterous play

_____

_____

Imaginative activities

_____

_____

Rituals (e.g. bed or bath time)

_____

_____

Jokes and fun

_____

_____

Secrets

_____

_____

Other

_____

_____

2 Are there marked differences between them in any of the following respects:

Examples

The roles they adopt

_____

_____

Activities and interests

_____

_____

Behaviour

_____

_____

Personality _____

_____

Other _____

_____

3 What evidence is there of reciprocity e.g.

Examples

Pride in each other _____

_____

Praise and criticism _____

_____

Mutual help _____

_____

4 Do they model on each other e.g.

Examples

Think they look alike _____

_____

Imitate each other _____

_____

Emulate the qualities they like _____

_____

Unite in face of problems _____

_____

Other _____

_____

5 Other observations on this relationship

_____

_____

6 What are these siblings' own views of their relationship? (views of other siblings can also be very illuminating).

_____

_____

_____

7 On the basis of all this evidence, sum up the positives and negatives that this relationship holds for each sibling

_____

_____

_____

_____

Date checklist completed _____

Name of person completing checklist _____

Relationship to the child _____

_____

_____